Letters

OF

ENDEARMENT

Letters
OF
ENDEARMENT

MELONDA A. PACE

XULON PRESS

Xulon Press
2301 Lucien Way #415
Maitland, FL 32751
407.339.4217
www.xulonpress.com

Unless otherwise indicated, Scripture quotations
taken from the King James Version (KJV) – *public
domain.*

Paperback ISBN-13: 978-1-66281-196-8
Ebook ISBN-13: 978-1-66281-197-5

Overture

"*I* am with you always!" This is God's undying commitment to us; but, do we really believe He is concerned with every passing second of our lives? We are never a distant memory, He is with us continuously. Often times, we are overwhelmed by the challenges of life. We neglect to invite Him into our daily activities and thoughts, that He may share with us His expertise on the vicissitudes of life. God wants to be completely involved in our lives. Even when we sleep He is caring for us. God loves and cares for us so much that He put it on my heart to write down these meditations for you, personally. He calls you His beloved in this collection of letters. Many have forgotten who He is. As He spoke thoughts of deity towards you, I warmly inscribed these "Letters of Endearment". May you never forget the passion God has for you, the apple of His eye.

From heaven into
your hearts
Enjoy!

Dear chosen one,

From thy mother's womb, I chose you to be a member of My royal priesthood. You were hand-picked — the best of the best. You were chosen to be part of the master plan. You are part of that chosen generation; just as My son Jesus was born for a specific reason, so were you.

As a prince and princess is groomed to be king and queen, I am grooming you, chosen one. No good thing will I withhold from those that will avail themselves to Me. I want you to see what I see, to hear what I hear, and to do what I do. I'm waiting on you. Soon you will see that I only have the best for you.

Earth, where I placed you, is full of My riches. I will give My riches to those who take their place in royalty. Chosen one, your eyes have not seen, nor your ears have heard, nor your thoughts can conceive the many good things I have for you — My chosen one.

With Love,

Jesus Christ

Single women,

*R*ejoice that you are single. Let your heart be Mine, to have and to hold, even after death. We will never part if you invite Me into your heart. You feel lonely; but you are really never alone. I am always with you; yet you push me away for the touch of a strong man hands. I reach out to you, but you turn and walk away. I want to whisper the sweet sound of truthful words to you; but, you are so caught up thinking that you are alone.

Single women, have you forgotten that I made you? I know how to quench your desires because I put them inside of you. Please do not be promiscuous and give yourself freely to other gods (men). When you learn to serve and be attentive to Me, then you will know Me when I walk in your presence and nothing else will matter. What your heart truly desires is our union — when I reach to hold you, and you run into My arms. Then you will praise Me for all I am to you and I will bless you for your sweet submission.

As you listen and obey My word (The Bible), fasten your eyes to My lips as if honey is dripping from them and you don't want to miss a drop. For when you learn to satisfy Me, the Creator first, then I will know I can trust and give you My creation man (your husband)

Sincerely,
God

Single men,

*M*en, you have misconstrued the idea of being single. You are the apple of My eye — My phenomenal creation. I have made you the head, a man of power and authority. I have made you a natural giver. I loved the world so; I gave my son, to provide for the world. <u>He endured the ultimate temptations;</u> yet He was a man of wisdom, not given to foolishness.

His desire was to please Me. Men, you are my prize possession. I have placed in your seed, not to sow as you please in every garden (woman) you meet. One apple seed brings forth a tree full of apples if you nourish it correctly. Listen wisely, what I have given you, do not abuse it. Seek Me with all your heart.

I will teach you as a single man how to prepare for your good thing (your wife). It's a beautiful thing to cultivate, love, honor, cherish, protect, and provide for the one garden (woman). In return, this garden will satisfy all of your needs. You can safely lay your head in her lap as she strokes your head. You will not need to worry whether she is a type of Delilah. Rather, you will know her as a delightful and pleasing woman to you as your wife.

In My Love,
Jesus Christ

Melonda A. Pace

Dear comfortless,

There is comfort for your soul. I am confident in the gift I left for you — the Holy Ghost. He the Comforter that the Father sent you. Take full advantage of Him. The Holy Ghost teaches all things.

I am here for you. I have the power to be whatever you want Me to be. Have you forgotten what I told Moses? I am that I am. I am rest for the restless and hope for the hopeless. I could go on telling you who I am, but you would run out of time.

Therefore, I will make it crystal clear; I'm the "<u>more</u>" to all of your "<u>less</u>". So, there is no need for you to feel comfortless in any circumstance. *"I will not leave you comfortless; I will come to you."* (John 14:18)

The Spirit of God

To My future glory,

There are many battles in this life between good and evil, many battles you have won, but the war is far from over. Spiritual "World War I" was won when I kicked Satan out of heaven, and when My son Jesus died on the cross and rose victoriously on the third day.

Presently, we are in spiritual "World War II", and it is all about you. Look at the big picture, Satan is fighting a battle he knows has already been won. He knows his final destination, he is trying to deceive you, and I am trying to retrieve you.

Satan knows you are going to become weary and wounded in this war, but don't you dare give up! Every battle you win is a slap in Satan's face. It reminds him that I've triumphed over him once again. Heaven is counting on you to be our future glory.

You must endure until the end which will be spiritual "World War III", when My son descends from heaven to rapture the saints. My future glory is for the one that endures until the end as a good solider. He/she will ascend with Me.

Don't give up my child, the suffering you're experiencing at this very moment will not compare to the future glory we shall have together forever. Be strong, I am with you.

*Your God
Mighty In battle*

Melonda A. Pace

Dear Inspiration,

o you dare to be a Daniel standing by God's purpose for his life, heeding God's commands? The plots of the enemy tried to pressure Daniel to compromise his faith and bend his principles. His life was often at risk, nevertheless, the enemy found him standing firm on My word.

When the powers that be decided to erect a statue and decree that Daniel could not pray to his God, they still found him praying to Me, the God of his salvation, the true living God.

They threw Daniel into the lions' den. I was so inspired by his faith that I dispatched angels to shut the mouths of the furious and hungry lions. Children of God, inspire Me with your faith, inspire Me with your prayers, inspire Me with your praise, inspire Me to do what the enemy says can't be done.

God

To My beloved,

I hear the questions asked in the agony of your flesh: Does Jesus really care when my heart is in pain? Does Jesus care when I have been rebuffed to no end? Does Jesus care about the many tears I cry at night until my pillow has become a pool of troubled water? Does Jesus care that I have forsaken all to follow Him?

Yes, My beloved, I care about your pain and tears. For these reasons and more, I overcame the world. I know you are cast down, but I care enough that I won't let you be destroyed.

Beloved, you ask do I care, I could be offended; but, I care enough to understand your human frustrations. I was once flesh too. Take a moment and reflect back on your life. Then, ask yourself, who else but God could have cared for me this much?

God Who cares!

Dear Clone,

To whom it concerns, I received a resounding and joyful message about an earthly being coming over to My side. Oh what joy came to Me when I knew that you were free! When you accepted Me in your life, you became a clone of my Son Jesus.

Looking from My heavenly view, I see that many don't understand how divinely they are made. When the first single blood cell of Christ touched your body you were reborn! It's in Me you live, move, and have your being. Your old spirit was washed away, and you became new.

Now you are My clone and are identical to Me. You have the capabilities of My character and power. You have it all inside of you. And guess what? The debt has already been paid. The only thing you have to do is accept My gift and use it to clone other souls for Me.

In My Love,
God

Dear servant,

I have given each of you special gifts, some apostles, prophets, evangelist, pastors, and teachers (Ephesians 4:11). My servants, I want you study and show yourselves approved unto me. Have patience and love that will never run out.

Walk worthy of the vocation to which you are called. It is not going to be easy, but I will make it worthwhile. <u>Develop a passion</u> for the gifts I have given you and be willing to die for My name sake.

There will be many afflictions of the righteous; but take comfort in knowing that I will deliver you from them all. The enemy shall attack you because of the ministry I have given you to tell the body of Christ and to the world.

My servant, be not dismayed whatever befalls you. Know that I, your God, will take care of you. I promise you will look back and say it was all worth it.

P.S.
fight the good fight of faith!

God

Find Your Resting Place

Dear servant,

I have seen you trying to find rest for your soul. You heard of a place where the wicked shall cease from troubling, and the weary shall be at rest, but that's after death. There is something you must find and master on this side of the Jordan while you are yet filled with mortal life. In this place you can find tranquility and repose in the middle of chaotic situations. You have no need to look any further because your search is over. You can find your resting place in sacred prayer with the God of Abraham, Isaac, and Jacob. For in this place, nothing can violate the sacred and holy place of God. In this place, communicate with Him honestly and He will communicate with you honestly. There is a level you can reach where you are rejoicing in hope even though you see things falling apart. In this place you will find rest continuously in sacred prayer. I can hide you from the enemy. It will become difficult for Satan to find anything to make you restless, simply because you have found the secret weapon for heavenly rest in this mortal life. Prayer.

Your God of Rest

Dear Valentine,

*T*his letter is only a mark of my love to you, for I have over 365 days of the year to show you how I love you, not just on the 14th day of February. For on that special day when you gave me your heart we became one for eternity.

My Valentine, I want you to know that I value our love. Every breath you take to give Me the fruit of your lips intoxicates Me. I am addicted to your praise. When you enter into worship, it takes me to a climax you can't even fathom in your earthly body.

My love can't be compared to human love, for I can truly take you far beyond ecstasy. I am the essence of love and I am dedicated to you. No one can change how I feel about you.

My Valentine, My love, have staying power. My love is always true, My love is healing to your sickness, shelter in your storm, and mender of your broken heart. My love is the lifter of your bowed head, My love is everything you need. Last, but far from being the least, My love shall take you from earth to glory where we shall bask in each other's presence forever. You are so much My Valentine.

From,
The Lover of your soul

Melonda A. Pace

IN THE MEANTIME

Dear servant,

My Father's children, I ask the question once again. Why stand here gazing? I know you are in between blessings (as you all say). You believe in Me, and I know you are looking and waiting for that miracle and the promises of God to come forth in your life; but while you are waiting, do yourself a favor:

In the meantime, praise Me!
In the meantime, love Me!
In the meantime, act like you know!
In the meantime, tell Me how awesome I am!
In the meantime, serve Me!
In the meantime, thank Me
In the meantime, show Me your faith!
In the meantime, tell Me how wonderful I am!
In the meantime, tell Me there is none like Me!
In the meantime, stand on My word!
In the meantime, let nothing shake your confidence!
In the meantime, Dance before Me like David did!
In the meantime, trust Me!
In the meantime, know it's already done!
In the meantime, pray and obey! You see it's all about what you do in the meantime.

Your God of Promise

BLIND SUBMISSION

My servant,

*B*lind submission is like getting on a roll-er-coaster for the first time blind folded or playing Russian roulette. It's a chance of possibly looking foolish to people that count you as a person of great wisdom, and going against common knowledge.

Obeying the Spirit isn't always popular. Moving on My command and not hearing from Me within a day or week (or even longer) concerning My command is difficult; yet you are steadfast, without a doubt, because you know you heard the Master's voice.

Your blind submission gives Me insight into your faith and confidence in Me. Don't be alarmed My child, you are not the first. Noah experienced blind submission when I told him to build the ark, people thought he was an old man losing his mind. After all, he was 600 years old; but his blind submission to the flooding power of God saved his life, and his family, and many of My creations. Walking in blind submission with Me is better than having perfect vision.

Jesus Christ,
Son of God

HE LIVES!!!

Dear servant,

*Y*ou can witness God's majesty by observing the
mountain top to the valley below; the depth of
the deep dark sea to the fowls that fly across the blue
sky; the blowing wind to the rising of the sun; the sap
of the trees to the splendor of grass. You can witness
God's majesty by observing the singing of the hum-
ming birds in the morning; the cold of winter to the
heat of summer; the shaking of the earth in California
and the red clay hills of Georgia. You can witness
Him in the blinking of your eyes to the beating of
your heart; the lifting of your hand to merely scratch
your head; every step you take to go where you please;
the person that has a fatal disease to a miraculous
healing; birth to death; the joyful sound of laughter
to the tears of sorrow; the faculty of your mind to
make a decisions to the changing of the same; and the
echo of sound in your ear. Mostly, you can Witness
the glory of God by meditating on Jesus' death on the
cross, to His rising from the tomb. Basically, He is in
the smallest detail to the largest thing you can ever see,
touch, hear smell, or taste. Know that it's only because
he lives (Jesus Christ)!

Jehovah

Dear abused woman,

$\mathcal{M}$any women are tolerating abuse in different ways, and this results in unhealthy thinking and living. I heard them when they said that you would always be a whore and that you would never amount to anything.

I know you have made many mistakes in your life and never recovered from all of them. You gave into the lie that a piece of a man is better than no man at all. You've allowed sexual, verbal, and physical abuse reduce your self-esteem. Manipulation has made you think you can't have God's best of anything.

I want you to know that you are My creation, woman. Besides, being wonderfully made, you possess a priceless treasure; you are a good thing, as My Word says. **Precious one, don't ever think you are beyond repair!**

Every breath you take is a chance for you to start over again. Know that if you never give Me a chance to show you who you can become, you will forever fall and believe anything. I am ready to give you strength to get up and repossess all of your jewels and place them back in your priceless treasure chest.

God the Potter

Dear abused men,

To my leaders, in order to lead you must allow Me to teach you. 99% of your abuse is mental. You have been taught wrongly and My heart cries out for you. It's not your fault how you were raised from a child to manhood.

I come with good news. I can change the wrong and make it right. First, you must lose that foolish pride, come to Me as a child and talk to Me one-on-one, don't be afraid to show Me your heart and tears.

I want to transform your mind, not abuse your masculinity or make you feel like the tail instead of the head. I dare not take back what I've given you. You are the head, but in order for you to lead you must allow Me to come in, that I may teach God's attributes of a man that leads.

I'm not the author of confusion, but the Prince of Peace. Don't let anyone confuse you, **men you don't have to live in captivity of your past abuse**. My teaching is simple with great results. If your teaching doesn't line up with Mine, it's all wrong!

Allow me to take out, and put in, for it will only make your life better! A better man, a better leader, a better lover, a better husband, a better father, a better friend, and better spiritually.

Your God of manhood

Dear Sacred,

To the single men and women who are virgins, don't feel disgraced. Virginity is a precious possession, something that is irreplaceable. You must not become embarrassed because you have restrained yourself. The greatest love story that has ever been told was not Romeo and Juliet, but when I gave My son. I could have created Him the way I did Adam and Eve, but instead I used a **virgin.** The world looks upon you and laughs, but maintaining your virginity is an honor. Don't be side-tracked by the jokes and distasteful talk about how many men or women have had relations outside of the confines of marriage. Don't give it a second thought when you are told you are missing out on a good thing. Understand Me clearly, sex is an invigorating and wonderful thing; however, you are not missing out on anything I have predestined for you to enjoy with your husband or wife at the set time. Truly, the only thing you're missing are: sexual diseases (which can be fatal) and soul ties that will cause you emotional torment. There is no authentic love or honorable pleasure in giving yourself to every person you lustfully desire. Hold to your sacredness.

Sincerely,
Jesus Christ

Melonda A. Pace

My sweet beauty,

I have made all things beautiful for My fulfillment; both the visible and invisible (even the thorns), everything was created by Me for My use and glory.

I made the outward appearance of mankind beautiful; but, there is a beauty that surpasses the frame of the flesh, a beauty that's pleasing to My eyes, ears, mind and heart.

I see beauty when you, a free agent, willingly choose to trust and depend on Me, considering so many choices you have in this world. The promises I've made to you haven't come to pass yet; but, I find a continuous praise coming from your lips and that's a sound of beauty to My ears.

My beautiful child, understand that genuine beauty is far past the outward appearance. Your inner beauty attracts My attention and captures My heart. Therefore, my heart desires desperately and passionately to shower you with My beautiful blessing from heaven above.

Truly yours,
The Lord

Dear servant,

hrough the many afflictions My bold servant the Apostle Paul encountered, he was undaunted; he was not intimidated by fear of persecution. I know you heard the famous and victorious story of how Paul and Silas were locked in jail and I shook the earth to set them free. My servant Paul was locked in jail many times, he was even under house arrest. He did not experience Me coming to his rescue in the same manner every time, he had to endure what I allowed, and trust Me to deliver him in My time. In his waiting, he had great joy before him that kept him focused. Paul focused on My death, which proved that God can take the darkest moment in history and bring good out of it. Therefore Paul was not focused on the dark times in his life, even when he knew that his time had come to die for My name sake. Instead, he focused on the resurrection, knowing that the Father would raise him up victoriously in the second coming of Christ. Learn the lesson from Paul and focus on Me, Jesus Christ, not the encounters that will come to test your faith in Me. For as I was with Paul, so I am now and will forever be a strong deliverer to those that trust in Me; because My focus is on you.

From Heaven's Best

Dear servant,

Every tear that falls from your eyes is a word to Me that brings forth a message from earth to heaven. Many have cried rivers of water. Don't be ashamed, even I wept. Let it all out, for I understand your tears just as My Father understood mine.

After you have cried, take a moment to dry your eyes and see My reflection of glory in your tears. For I have sent an angel down to bless your troubled water. So My dear, whatever it is that's causing your heart to ache, all you need to do is step in faith and be made whole, as the glory of your tears will be revealed.

The King of Glory

TAKE ANOTHER LOOK

My Love,

Take another look and see through My eyes, the eyes of God. I know what you see looks bad. I see the circumstances you see; but, do you see what I see? Come take My hand, step out of your present time situation, and stroll with Me into the future, because what your present looks like now is unlike your future. My love, stop panicking and take another look. Don't despise the making and molding of the great man or women of God I'm creating you to be. Right now you are gold in the rough; I must put you in the fire in order to make you My finest.

Christ

IMAGE

My child,

Often, I hear you say to yourself, I am not important, I'm just here until the Lord takes me home. You are <u>little</u> in your own eyes, and others eyes too. There is nothing I have made that is insignificant; <u>little</u> becomes much when you place it in My hands.

David was <u>little</u> in the eyes of Goliath, the philistine giant, but the image of Me inside David was greater than these: Goliath, the lion, the bear, and the thousands of men he slew.

The stones were smaller than both David and Goliath, but when David picked up the <u>little</u> stones, they became so much more when he placed them in My hands. His stature was small, but his image and faith in Me was stupendous.

Your image is greater than what you see in the mirror, for you are the image of Me. I am more than a conqueror, and so are you. Place your image in My hands — little, fat, skinny, educated or not, however you see yourself — put it in My hands and watch your image become so much. more.

God
Image Consultant

Dear Down & Out,

There is a lifting for you. I speak to the sun every morning and say "rise". I say unto you there is a lifting for you, now is the time, don't hold your head down in despair any longer, for I am Jesus the lifter of your head.

Lift up your head and see My glory work for you, lift up your head and see the resplendent majesty and beauty of My notability, lift up your head! I speak to you today! It is your time to experience heavenly bliss and splendor on My earth.

If indeed you must bow your head, let it be to worship and praise Me for the lifting I have begun in you.

From God Who Cares

EMPTY

Dear great one,

Come before Me and worship as an empty vessel. Come before Me in the spirit of truth. Many anointed ministries I have given My servants have caused many to feast, and fill their souls through evangelist, Prophets, Pastors, Singers, etc.

You are depleted. You are in need of a refill from Me. It's a dangerous thing to minister on fumes. Come to Me and worship Me for what I have done through you.

It is I, the Lord, that have made you, not yourselves. The adversary comes so easy to make you think other wise. I know the secret things with which you struggle. I do not mean to threaten, but to keep you humble; it's My good pleasure to prosper you in every area of your life.

Don't become polluted in greatness and fame. Always come before Me empty of pride, self-righteousness and anything that exalts itself above Me. Come that I may fill you over and over again with My righteousness that you might continue to **be great in Me.**

Humbly yours,
Christ

Dear servant,

This is a treacherous combination that will bring you to the lowest common denominator in no time flat. It will take you far away from your original call of duty.

In the process of training, My disciples become caught up in the Knick-Knack-paty-whack of who was the greatest among them, not concentrating on current events.

How long will you simple ones love your simple ways? You must flee from this type of behavior. I have given you ministry to bring forth, skill and favor that will put you in high places so that you may spread My good news.

My child, you are caught up in the knick-knack-paty-whack. You may be thinking, why me? I work hard and no one acknowledge me. I can't do this because of my past sins. Or you are concerned of what others think of you. You are fasting and praying in vain trying to appear more spiritual than others. Oh my child, come up higher, get beyond this bad behavior and redeem lost time. There are higher heights and deeper depths I desire to take you to.

God

Dear Clueless,

Who am I? I'm the wind that parted the Red Sea, the stone that killed Goliath, protection for Daniel in the lions den, Elijah's fire, the widow women's everlasting bread, Esther's courage, Solomon's wisdom, the healing hem for the woman with the issue of blood, Jehoshaphat's army of angels, and the fire consumer for the three Hebrew boys. I am the great God almighty strong in battle. Dear confused, I am greater than a military defense, none on earth is My equal, and to everyone that believeth, I fortify physically, mentally, and spiritually, which makes them certified defenders of the universe. I am a mighty fortress, the only force to be reckon with. This is just a little clue to you of who I am.

God Almighty

SALVATION

Dear servant,

My precious one, you may have been raised in a different religion. Many have never seen the inside of a church; because they were taught there is no God nor a heaven or hell.

The world is filled with many denominations; but if they go against My word (The Bible) it's not authentic. Just as sure as you are reading this letter there is a heaven and a hell.

Precious one, I don't fault you for your upbringing. My Father did not bring Me into the world to condemn it; but that the world through Me, Jesus Christ, might be saved. (John 3:16, 17)

Now that you are older, I ask you to give Me a chance. I know you may have doubts; but trust Me. Salvation is My forte, prove Me now and ask Me to come into your heart. I've been waiting so long for this moment. I prepared Myself for this moment many years ago.

Try me against any other gods you know, and I will make a shame of them openly, there is no other name (gods) under the heaven given among men whereby you can be saved. Come to Me and ask Me to save you.

Yours truly,
The God of your salvation

Melonda A. Pace

Dear servant,

I have been looked upon many ways, looked passed, looked over, looked around and looked under. When will you look at Me face to face and realize that I am the source? If you grew wings and flew to the utmost part of the earth you would find Me there. If you went to the deepest part of the sea, surely I would be there. I am high and lifted up, you can't fly over Me. I take My morning strolls in the depths of the sea, there is no place you can hide from God. Listen, I don't play games, therefore automatically I'm disqualified from playing hide-n-seek, I am the source you need from a to z…

a-answer	n-nourisher
b-brother	o-obligated
c-creator	p-passionate
d-direction	q-quicken power
e-everlasting	r-resourceful
f-friend	s-sage
g-good	t-truthful
h-healer	u-understanding
I-interceder	v-valorous
j-justified	w-worthy of honor
k-king of kings	x-cross out your sins
l-liable	y-yearning to love you
m-master of	z-zealous to bless you everything

I am all this and more

Your Source

Loved Ones From Heaven

Dear servant,

This letter comes from the thoughts and prayers of the family and friends who are with Christ in heaven. They are not as you remember, for they have been changed from the mortal to the immortal. They are filled with joy unspeakable.

As they look down and pray for you, they asked Me to whisper in your ears and tell you that heaven is worth it all. Heaven is not a fairy tale, it's living well without the horror of hell. They want you to know that it's imperative that you do right in the sight of God.

They want you to let go of the sins that bind you, because if you only had a glimpse of half of heaven, you wouldn't give the temptation of sin a second thought. Sin would be like the dirt under your feet.

Your family and friends would say "We did not do enough for God to have given us such heavenly magnificence". So think it not robbery to give God 100% of your service, because every test, everything you give up for Christ sake is worth it all.

P.S. We are in preparation to come back with Jesus soon!

Sincerely
Yours truly

Joy of Jesus

To My temporary joy child,

Make Me, Jesus, your joy — not your car, home, money or people. For these things only bring temporary joy and satisfaction. When it all fades, you are like a ship without a sail. Anchor your joy in Me, Jesus.

Those who master making Me the center of their joy are not easily moved when misfortunes happens. If they are moved at all, it will be to their knees to pray.

In My Love,
J. C.

My Love,

My servant, you have been praying a long time asking me to do certain things in your life. You get up from praying, and give Me thanks for the manifestation, thanking Me for those things that are not as though they were.

Many of your petitions I have brought to pass. Now you wonder where are the other things for which you've prayed? You ask, "Have you heard me Lord?" Yes! My servant, I have heard you.

I have showered down blessings and put them in place; but My question to you is, where are you? You keep saying the devil is holding your blessings. That's not true. There are things I have told you to do, and places I have told you to go, and you chose not to obey.

Little did you know that the answer to your prayer was there in the things you refused to do. My child, get in place and receive the fullness of all I have for you.

Jehovah Jireh

Melonda A. Pace

Greatness,

I planted a small seed of greatness in your heart when you were born. As you grew and reached the age of maturity, I told you it was there. You ask, "when did you tell me Lord?" Well, when you turned on the television and heard the preacher say "God has a plan for your life". When you walked into the church for the first time on Easter Sunday with your grandparents and the morning hymn was "How Great Thou Art". When you thoughtlessly picked up a book and flipped through the pages to a chapter entitled "Greatness". That was My subtle way of speaking to you.

The seed of greatness I have planted in you has the power to give you every good thing earth has to offer (even surpassing Mars, Saturn, Pluto, Jupiter) into a place where only the great can abide. Don't smother your seed with doubt, don't drown it with tears of sorrow, nourish it with faith, don't let Satan's deceiving weeds choke the life out of your seed, praise Me and watch Me destroy the strong hold of Satan. My child, maximize the minimum with the greatness inside of you

The Father

Dear cherished,

*O*n the sea of life, it's hard to see the truth because it's so cloudy and the clouds are so low that you can hardly make a distinction between the clouds and the sea. You are overwhelmed with so many wrong turns that the angry sea has caused you to take.

I challenge you to make the right turn, which is to Me. Rest on My raft of hope. You are worn out and you can't fight any longer. Your raft of hope will cause you to float instead of remaining immobile because your arms are too tired to make another stroke, and your legs can't kick any longer.

It seems like life's waves are 10 feet tall; but grab to hold God's out-stretched hands as Peter did in Matthew 14:33. He will cause your storm to cease. When the waters are calm, you will see that what you thought were wrong turns caused by the storm will bring you to a new horizon on My raft of hope.

God of Hope

Beloved,

*I*n case you forgot, I decided to make man because I thought it was good. It's amazing how quickly you forget your Creator and believe your life is your own. Just in case you have forgotten, I want to remind you of the small and the great. Remember when people were being raped in your community? I placed angels around you and your house. Every time you laid down to sleep and rose the following morning, I allowed it to be. Every breath you expect to be there when you inhale was Me. Remember when your child was in the classroom and a student began shooting? Many were wounded, some even died; but your child came out, frightened, but alive I covered your child with my right hand.

Remember that day you were held at gun point by a group of youngsters just wanting to see someone die? I, God, stayed the hand of death. Beloved, I know some of these things you think were by chance or luck; but, let Me tell you it's been Me all the time. Yes, that summer night hanging out with friends on the porch, minutes before a deadly drive-by, I caused you to have a desert thirst. You went into the house to quench your thirst. That was Me saving your life. I'm not boasting, I just want you to know your Creator, the God of Israel, who never slumbers is watching over you because you are His beloved. I know you have a tendency to forget, I understand you are only human. This is why this letter was written, just in case you forgot.

J. Christ

To you,

I challenge you to devote this letter to memory and recite it every day with faith as a grain of a mustard seed. Recite it specifically when you feel a little faint. Declare it!

Say this: My spirit will not be moved, I stand steadfast and abiding in the fact that Jesus rose with all power on the third day with me in mind. I am His and therefore I possess that same power. I stand on God's word. Everything He conquered, I can conquer. The wealth He possesses, I possess in my life. I shall live in abundance in every area of my life because I believe.

Your God of
Life Abundantly

Melonda A. Pace

VERTICAL UP LIFT

Dear servant,

If you sow into the heavens, I will sow into the earth. No matter what is going on in the horizontal always give Me vertical praise, (not just a typical clapping of your hands and a one "thank you Jesus" with your mouth). Give Me a heartfelt praise of gratitude, with a good attitude, because your good attitude affects your altitude. It lifts you up from the horizontal situations (earthly cares) and puts you in a vertical position. In a vertical position, your spirit connects to God's spirit. Try this, the next time you open your mouth to murmur, fill your mouth with praise. I make My home in your praise. Know that in your vertical up-lift (praise) will dispel everything that's tormenting your life. Let God arise in vertical praise and your problems will be deciphered in the horizontal.

Build Me a Home of Praise,

God

My True Love,

We are a match made in heaven. As you go through this mandated life, I am waiting to hear your voice. I am listening to hear your special request that I may go to the Father and make intercession for you.

There are months when I don't hear from you and it causes my heart to ache. I am in love with you, don't stay away from Me, even in those times you don't know what to say, come to Me in moaning and groaning that only I, God, can understand.

I'm waiting for the love of My life. You know how it is being in love with someone. You don't have to say anything, just being in their presence satisfies your heart. I'm longing to be in My lover's presence.

Lay aside those weights that are keeping you from Me. What's more important than Me, your heavenly lover? I'm the one that speaks and everything must obey, the one that hangs the sun in the morning to shine on your wonderful face, and the moon at night to softly calm all your cares of the day.

I have more benefits for you than the stars you can count. There is truly no good thing I will withhold from you My true love. Come and indulge in my heavenly affection.

Yours Truly!

To disbelief,

To the nations of disbelief, this is a letter of true prophecy. Suddenly, news will flash across the world saying, "A major panic has swept the nation". Operator 9-1-1 lines will be lit up like fireworks on the Fourth of July.

Cheaters creeping to be with their lovers will be astounded by the sight of driverless vehicles crashing in the streets. Loved ones will suddenly disappear from families sitting watching television

Graves will be opened, pilots will disappear in mid-flight, husbands and wives asleep in bed will discover their spouse is missing. It's declared world-wide that it's an alien abduction, because the drama can't be explained with common sense.

People will try to kill themselves, radio stations everywhere will hear a sound in the air that's disrupting their programs, sounding like a shout of praise and music in the air.

Suddenly, people will begin to remember the witness from saved loved ones. They will realize they have been left behind, because of disbelief. Tell Me, on which side of the rapture will you be?

The soon coming King

Dear child,

I know you thought this time would never come in your life, I had to stretch you. I heard you say I was stretching you like a rubber band and you were wondering if it would ever break. You became weary of hearing the same prophecies, you were as good as comatose to prophecy, it was a cliché to you.

Now I hear your sweet sigh as you sit back and relax in your dream-house furnished with the finest of everything. I see your thankful tears as they fall on your silk pillow. I hear your prayer asking the Lord to bless someone tomorrow; all because I (God) have stretched you to millionaire status.

You are traveling first-class. Go and minister to My people. The only debt you have is to praise Me forever. I need you to testify and be strong for your sisters and brothers in Christ, who are in the process of My stretching.

God

My soldier,

Why do you like playing in the minefield? Surely you know there is a war going on. I have given you basic training, you know how to go on the enemy camp ground and retrieve all he has taken from you; but tell me why are there times I look for you and you are absent without honorable discharge?

You have your sword in your hand, you are adorned in full armor, but your mind is set on doing things your way. You are sleeping with the enemy, dinning at the enemies table eating the finest foods, that's laced with destruction.

You are so smart that you don't think you need all of what I taught you in basic training any more, mainly because you want to please your no-good flesh. My soldier, come out of the minefield before I remove My heavenly host from around you and allow the enemy to consume you.

Your General

Whazup Shawdi

Yo, I've seen your rap, the gang banging, you're just a little Bonnie and Clyde, huh, getting your high from wheeling, dealing, steeling, and killing. The mention of your name brings terror to others, and that gives you a thrill. Check this, I am God and I am everywhere at all time, how cool is that I see you when all the gang is gone. I have the power to see straight through you.

I see the cause of your derangement; the misery and tears after you have come down from your fatal highs. I speak to you and you think you are still tripping, naw you aint tripping! It's Me Jesus Christ waiting to save you from yourself.

You begin to feel Me, then you shake it because you don't like the feeling of not having control, so you harden your heart against Me. It's cool, My love aint like the others that pushed you to this place, My love suffers long, it's kind and patient, My love for you had Me killed, on the real, check the Holy B (Bible)

Shawdy, soon as you realize your arms are too short to box with Me (God), your guns can't kill Me, and your name don't shake me, you will give Me the con, the control to make you more powerful than you have ever been, slick I know you like power.

Oh, don't worry about the gang, once they see how smooth I've made you, fa sho they gone peep my power to see what's the dealeo and guess what, it's gone be off the he-z-fa-she-z. See you on the flip side (my side).

Big J.C

Melonda A. Pace

To my one man army,

Every day is a day of happiness, it is simple as speaking to your mind. Say to yourself every morning, today is my day of happiness. Did you know your mind a lone is a powerful force? It can take you anywhere in the world without taking a step or packing a suitcase, all you have to do is think on it.

There are challenges you face daily, but you can choose how they will affect you. Your mind is so strong that it gives order to the entire body; it dictates whether you will be happy or sad. Build a wall around your mind with my scripture.

"Finally, brethren, whatsoever things are true, whatsoever things are honest, whatsoever things are just, whatsoever things are pure, whatsoever things are lovely, whatsoever things are of good report: if there be any virtue, and if there be any praise, think on these things." (Philippians 4:8)

Every day can truly be a day of happiness. Search your vicinity. If you can't find any of the Philippians' attributes above, dismiss it any bring it under your command. Control it don't let it control you. Your mind is a one man army.

God

Xenia's in this world,

ne year in the month of August 31st, I created another wonderful child. Her parents named her Xenia and was a sweet, caring, and compassionate child. She had an honest persuasion that the pure affection she gave to everyone would be returned. Many people couldn't see her as a model because of her full-figured body, but she was a model of My beauty. Some people thought she was unsuccessful, but she succeeded in teaching My ultimate reason of being – which is love. Xenia was a habitual mortal that duplicated the essence of the love of My son, Jesus Christ. Tell Me: why does one work so hard to be accepted by mere flesh? You work overtime to receive approval of someone that's exactly like you; but without Me all of you would be useless. The human race and its artificial distinctions with weight, color, money, education, and appearance, for when you ostracize another I (God) have created, you do it unto Me, and I shall repay. <u>Think for a moment how ludicrous it is for you to allow your equal to make you feel absent of the perfection of beauty I have given you.</u> Xenia's aunt wrote her a letter to keep with her, stating this fact. Nonetheless, this sweet angel departed this life with a broken heart.

This is why I write to you, my wonderful creation, young or old, for when indeed you encounter someone that attempts to oppose who I say you are

— know that it's your radiant light beaming on their insecurities. But don't leave them blinded by your light — open their eyes that they may see the truth, that I (God) don't make anything ugly or useless, and welcome them into the organization, the A.B.G.C. (Accepted By God Club). In memory of Xenia

God

Dear Servant,

I write this letter you, because I want you to comprehend Philippians 4:13: that you can <u>absolutely</u> do all things through Christ Who strengthens you. This is one of the most powerful scriptures in the Bible, as this scripture gives capacity to My mastery strength, yet it is ever taken so lightly.

Release your mind of everything at this very moment, and focus on this scripture. I want to bombard you with muscle of My strength, that's available to you. My strength is a miraculous intervention moving for earthly vessels.

Christ, by anyone's account, is the most significant person who ever lived the supreme revelation of God's strength. His strength breaks down the immune system of the impossible and makes all things possible for the one that believes.

Let My strength be great inside of you working outward as a testimony where it is possible to do all things. When man mixes faith with the strength of God, one can do anything.

Your God of
Miraculous Strength

Melonda A. Pace

Dear parents,

I send you this letter of encouragement, being a parent is a crucial assignment. I give you a small innocent life to shape and form to embrace the world. You have the power to put good or evil into this child and I have trusted you with that task.

Broken marriages, single parents, whatever state you are in, you must never forget that you are a teacher (A parent teaching your child), from the womb to delivery and from delivery to day-one and beyond.

You must not allow your hurts to corrupt the precious miracle; but find a way to transform the negative into the positive. Remember with me all things are possible, teach the rewards of choosing to love instead of hate.

Take time to answer their questions that seem so simple to you. Don't push them away for you are your child's greatest teacher. Don't make them think learning is obsolete. Above all, teach them about Me, Jesus Christ.

Let your child know that you don't have all the answers; but, you know someone who does. Assure them that I am the answer, not drugs, sex, alcohol and violence. Teach them how to pray to Me, because I will always be there.

The Greatest Teacher,
Jesus Christ

Dear Creation,

*R*evelations 4:11 declares, "*Thou art worthy, O Lord, to receive glory and honor and power for thou has created all things, and for thy pleasure they are and were created.*"

Pay attention to the word <u>"all" in the scripture above</u>. It means total existence of every creature which is in heaven and on the earth, and under the earth, and such as are in the sea, all nations are my creation.

To everything there is a season, and a time to every purpose under the heaven, a time to be born, and a time to die, a time to laugh, and a time to cry, I know the most difficult thing on earth to deal with is death.

Loosing someone your heart has woven together in love is painful. You suddenly realize they are no longer on the earth when you reach for the phone, or take a breath to call their name.

You ask why, and I don't mine answering, but many of you cross the line of Creator and creation. If I allowed a tornado to up-root every tree I created, it's My choice. It's not good to ask as if you were the creator, and I the creation,

Everything I've given and will give to you (family, friends, and all the pleasures of life) I, God, <u>share</u> it with you for a season that you may enjoy My creating pleasure. Understand that when that season is up, don't say I'm being unfair, but thank Me for the time and season I allowed you to share

God the Creator

Special one,

*M*any have laid down so casually at bedtime and took their last breath. Some have even taken a quick nap in the middle of the day, set their alarm clock for 30 minutes and slipped away forever. Someone went to the corner store to get milk for their cereal, but a drunk driver hit them, paralyzing them instantly and put them in a coma. Or a fatal stray bullet hits you. Now I want you to stop and think about what you have read (now read it again).

Right here is your present day. Ask yourself what you can do to make the rest of this day a day of happiness. At sunset, ask yourself whether you did everything to make this a day of happiness for you and others. You can sleep better not regretting your day and then you won't be reluctant to face tomorrow.

Because with the help of God you can find happiness in your everyday walk with Me. Believe it or not, happiness is all around you. Even in your worst times, when things look unfavorable, dictate to yourself (and everything around you) that today is your day of happiness.

P.S. Rejoice and be exceedingly glad!

Jesus Christ

Dear servant,

efore you speak, think, will this edify God, the ear that is listening? Will my words be filled with life or death? When you speak, will it be words of prayer for your brother or sister in Christ? Words are powerful, the cliché words don't hurt is one of the greatest lies that has ever been told. If I, your Father, spoke evil, and doubt to you all the time it would deteriorate your self-esteem and even your thoughts of heaven. As a matter of fact, you might think you would rather go to hell. You would think there is no hope. My child, think about the question, Where is hope? Thus says the sinner, the pregnant teenager, and young father, the person in the church that's about to give up, and the person that thinks suicide is the only answer. Being that your are not God, you don't know the day, time or hour when one of the persons above may be in the presence of your words. When you speak, will your words have the power to change a life for the better? You never know when I'm depending on you. It may be in the privacy of your home, where your unbelieving spouse and children may be, listening to your conversation about your job, or on the phone. I know you want to vent about the things that bother you. That's why I'm here. Talk to me the, Master conversationalist. Cast all your cares on Me, that you may be clear to minister words of life to others. Do you know that the enemy listens to your words, if it's bad he goes to perform it, if it's good, he goes to block it. Be wise and speak life that's where I live.

God Who Listens

Melonda A. Pace

Great warriors,

This war is day in and day out. Believe it or not, your soul is under siege from birth to death. Because of sin, you are born and forced to make choices. My word reads in Matthew 6:24: *"No man can serve two masters, choose ye this day whom you will serve."* When you accept Me in your heart you are born again. You were born with all you need to win this war. I (God) have given you a killer instinct, to put to death, nullify and cancel any and everything that comes against Me. Yes, I am a killer and a consuming fire, I told you in My word I am many things. If you don't know then you had better read My word. I've given you the command to slaughter for your survival and food (the bread of life, The Bible). The Bible is your guide to win this war. Ask for My anointing to make your instincts keen and sharpen your senses. You are to destroy anything that tries to alter My word in your life before it contaminates you. Don't be passive and foolish, your enemy is trying to take you out. Therefore, I give you the power to fight back by any means necessary to survive in this fallen world. You don't need a gun, knife, balm or any physical weapon; let me show you what the power of prayer, believing and obeying can do.

God of War

Trading Places

Cherished one,

re you ready to trade the sorrows of this world for a life time of pleasure? Are you ready to trade your body that needs to be fixed, operated on and adjusted, for a body that will forever be perfected? Imagine a place where you don't have to look over your shoulders, a place you don't have to constantly fight your adversary, but only experience heavenly peace.

It's yours, I have already prepared this for you, My cherished ones; however, you must be wise as a serpent, because the prince of the world comes to pressure you to trade places. He wants you to trade your love for Christ to hate, he wants you to trade your 10 to 30 minute prayer time to no time at all, and he wants you to trade your faithfulness to church to having a television Pastor that can't watch for your soul.

Satan wants you to think I have deceived you. I am not the liar, he is. He has already traded his place as chief musician for a place of eternal domination. Think about it, do you really want to trade your life for the worst>

Jesus Christ

Dear servant,

I address you in matchless love. The wrong choice has landed you in this place of confinement. Friends have fallen away like leaves on a perfect fall day. Your family doesn't understand; yet they love you anyway, even when you zoomed past all of their warning signs.

I'm not angry with you, now I have your undivided attention behind the bars of a jail cell. I said, I would never leave you nor forsake you, and I meant just that, since you chose this way, I must go with you.

Therefore, you don't have the right to die on me. I dare you try to end the life I gave you. When I'm ready for it to end, I will take it. My will shall be done through your life. Allow me to transform your mind in this awful place.

Let Me specialize in the impossible through you. Please My child, don't break my heart any more. Change the world you are in by rehabilitating lives, bringing women and men that are incarcerated to Me (Christ). Let them know they are not forgotten.

We are in this cell together; you need Me now, more than ever. Just as I was calling you to witness for Me before you were incarcerated, I am still calling you to do the same thing now. You can't faint now. I still have souls to save through your witness of Me in this place.

God

Dear refreshing,

Why dine on yesterday's bread when you have a foe that plans new strategies every day to grasp you in his evil clutches? I told you to ask Me for your daily bread and I will give it to you fresh from heaven. It's sad to have access to release a refreshing in your life, and never be asked for it. In case you have forgotten, I am the bread of life! He that hunger and thirst after Me shall be filled. I'm ready to refresh the old and make new. You believing in Me puts the yeast in the bread, and causes Me to arise in every circumstance in your life. I am your God that daily loads you with benefits.

The Bread of Life

Melonda A. Pace

Precious one,

You don't have to be the greatest evangelist, missionary, pastor, or singer in the world. You don't have to be the author of a bestselling book or have the finest education money can buy. You don't need to be a leader in the church or a member of the millionaire club. Remember, I was popular, and I was treated like the under-dog. All you need is just enough faith to believe I am who I say I am. I am Jehovah-Rapha, the Lord that healeth thee; Jehovah-Jireh, the Lord who provides; and Jehovah-Nissi, the Lord who is your banner of victory. I will show you great and mighty things.

Lord of All

Dear servant,

I was looking down from heaven viewing a funeral service one Saturday afternoon. There was a wise young man who spoke so profoundly the sentiments of My heart in these words: "No matter what you go through in life, God always fixes it. You must give Him praise". When, indeed, you find yourself in a place like Job — praise Me. If you were born with perfect vision and something happens that causes you to lose your sight — praise Me. If you lose an arm or leg — praise Me. I hear you say, "God are you serious?" I am as serious as your next breath. In every situation, after you have endured an emotional explosion, praise waits for you.

God,
The Giver of Praise

Stay Intact

Dear servant,

Relationship is a natural association that helps the world go around. It's one of the sweetest things to have a relationship with the opposite gender; but don't lose yourself, don't throw away your ambitions. This has happened too many times when a man meets a woman and they find common ground and companionship in one another. It's two individual lives that are now intertwined which means, I have a two person plan that needs to be executed. I'm not saying that, in the future, the two can't be joined together in matrimony; but, whatever may become of the situation, you must stay intact. I'm going to share with you the spiritual side of relationship. He has found you, (his good thing), as I planned and you both know that this is My will! I have seen this too many times. . What if one decides in the relationship that he or she is not going to obey the will of God? Would you stay intact? Because the enemy is fighting against everything I have ordained to be, from the smallest to the biggest concerning your life. You can't lose it, I need you to stay intact, because there is nothing more important than our relationship together.

Dear frustrated,

It's been a long time since I heard from you, yes, I've been watching and waiting. You keep doing the same thing over and over, and it's not working. In your frustration you ask, Lord why isn't it working? Before I can answer you, you began to do the same thing over again. If only I could get you to give Me the things you can't handle; better yet, give Me the things you think you can handle, because I can always do it better! Dear frustrated, don't go through any crazy changes, just start acknowledging Me in all of your ways.

God,
Who Knows All

Melonda A. Pace

Divine choices,

Life's choices are destined to be made, what will I eat today, will I wear red or green, these choices are part of life. A sweet woman waiting for love and wealth meet two gentlemen with the same name, Adam. Swayed by the wealth of them both, it wouldn't be a bad choice either way. Little did she know the Father watching the scene from a distance knew she was in trouble because she didn't even ask his advice. Thirsting to know them both, her weekends were never slow. The first Adam became corrupted. He became caught up in his wooing and soothing her with his cunning sweet words. He wanted to bring low, he was frying her brain with cocaine, their relationship became insane. She was taught good morals, but she was giving them up at any cost. She thought there was no way out; surely this would be her demise. Suddenly, the second Adam came in, strong and mighty and restored her life again. Needless to say she fell in love with him that day. He took her to heights unknown and showed her love that quivered her to the bone. He gave her wealth far beyond all she could ever ask or think. She asked herself, what did I do to deserve all of this? He drew her to his breast and said to her so passionately, it was your divine choice.

We will forever have to make choices between the two men in our lives. They both can give us what our flesh desires — love wealth, and pleasure. Will you choose Adam the corruptible, or Adam the incorruptible? Remember, the choice will determine to your final destination; so choose wisely.

God,
The Better Choice

*To My pursuer
of success,*

The success of My general, Joshua, was totally in his personal obedience to My will. He was to meditate on it, which means to ponder, read aloud and re read daily.

Joshua's obedience to Me made him a genius on the battlefield. His prudence allowed him to take the first step well and not stumble at the threshold of victory of obtaining God's promised land.

Those that faithfully acknowledge God in their ways will be guided with His wisdom to success. Because He is the master mind of everything, in Joshua chapter 6, He wages the first psychological warfare in history, the science of mental process.

God confounded Joshua's enemies minds before they could even lay a hand on them, they were weak minded. They had heard about the many great successes of Joshua's God.

I will do the same for you My love, read Joshua 1:8 and believe it!

The God of Joshua

THE EX-HARLOT

Dear servant,

In her sin, her faith in God was more powerful than many of the Israelites who watched as God divided the Red Sea so they could walk on dry ground. She had more faith than the Israelites who followed the pillar of a cloud by day and fire by night, and ate manna from heaven.

This ex-harlot was included in the messianic line. She was blessed of those that have not seen and yet believed. Don't allow your transgressions stop you from believing that God doesn't reward people that have faith in Him (whether saved or not). I caution you not to stop at believing, but invite God to come into your life and watch Him make you better than ever. Rahab believed, but, after she saw the protection and victory of My mighty hands, she gave herself to the greatest Man she had ever experienced — Me.

God

To all my Father's Children

Dear servant,

This letter comes with great joy from heaven! Our Father is sending Me to come and gather you all very soon. Hold on stronger to your faith in God. Believe Me when I tell you that everything you have gone through on earth will be made worth it in heaven.

Last but not least, thank you for not taking My suffering and dying for you for granted. I am so excited about you all coming home where you will experience what our Father wanted life to be from the beginning.

Be strong and of a good courage!

Jesus Christ
The Son of God

To whom it may concern,

(Please say your name in the blanks below)

I, the Lord, know your thoughts, and while pondering them in My mind; I was interrupted by a few people:

Daniel said, my Lord, tell _____ the God we serve caused me to be thrown into the lions den; but; Jehovah Shammah was <u>present</u> through His angels that shut the mouths of the lions.

Then someone else said "excuse me, may I speak a word my Lord?" Job said, "tell _____ our God took everything from me for a season, not because of a penalty for sin; but, because He believed in me, the way He's believing in _____ right now. When my testing was complete, Jehovah Jireh, <u>provided</u> everything I lost for His sake — twice as much.

Next, a beautiful fragrance filled the air, and a soft spoken voice said, oh, my Sweet Lord and Savoir may I share a word with _____ on earth? Tell _____ I was willing to perish for what I believed about our God, but He wouldn't let it be, He favored me and my people. Tell _____ the favor of God is with him/her, and the saints are on the altar praying for his/her strength.

_____ I, the Lord, wants you to know that there are more prayers for you than those that are against you. The race is given to the one that endures to the end. Fight the good fight of faith _____.

God

Dear hurting,

I'm going to make this short and powerful, because sometimes there are moments in life where you don't need a Sunday morning sermon, but a quick fix.

I know you just experienced something that was so hurtful to you; but I, your Father up above, want you to realize that yes, it's hurtful **but not paralyzing**. You must keep moving on toward your destiny I have for you. **Now Go Forth In The Name Of Jesus!**

God

Melonda A. Pace

Dear servant,

Don't get caught up in the <u>artificial blessings</u>, which are the many material things people will give you and the sweet accolades that will flow from their mouths like honey. In doing so you will miss the <u>Authentic Blessings</u> of God, which are a greater anointing (insight in the Spirit and a greater power to do greater works to edify the body of Christ).

Remember, give it all back to Me, what I've done for you, what I will do through you — give it all back to Me. You can't keep My glory for yourself! It belongs to Me and no one else.

The more you humble yourself and realize that it's in Me you live, it's in Me you have your being then the more I will use you. I will use you because you understand if it had not been for Me (The Lord) on your side, you couldn't even say a decent grace over you food.

Most of all preach the gospel at all time and only use words when necessary! This means let your life-style preach before you open your mouth to say anything.

Your Humble Servant

Dear Human,

"For my thoughts are not you thought, neither are your ways my ways", you will find these words in Isaiah 55:8. This is the authentic truth, there is a colossal dissimilarity between My mind (God) and your mind (human).

Allow me to share a true story with you, in Atlanta Georgia on April 28th between 12 and 1:30 am, I allowed a tornado to destroy a church named Rehoboth Deliverance Center Church of God in Christ.

Now, the human mind would say, clear everyone out of the church so no one will get hurt and die; but, God's mind decided to demonstrate 3 miracles to Georgia. All three persons walked out of a church that was torn to pieces. What a mighty God I am!

Many negate that fact, rushing to say "Oh my God, they must not have been living right"; but, that's the human mind talking. God (laughing out loud), sometimes I allow things to happen whether a person is good, bad, saint or sinner. You can always be sure whatever, I, God allows to happens, **My purpose is always to get everybody's attention. Do I have yours yet?** My son Jesus suffered and died on the cross because He did what wrong? NOTHING. It would be a great idea if the humans would let me be God.

Melonda A. Pace

To my light,

hy are you so amazed when you encounter dark times in your life? Matthew told you to let your light so shine before men, that they may see your good works, and glorify Me, your Father which is in heaven, (Matthew 5:16).

I put my light (you) in darkness to shine a path of righteousness to the one that is in darkness to help them find their way out.

Be patient, I have no intention of leaving you in darkness. I, God, will perform whatever is necessary to assure both your entrance and exit of those that are Mine.

God

WHEN JESUS SPEAKS!

Dear servant,

I know you are crying because you are frustrated and hurting deeply within because you are waiting on a particular prayer to be fulfilled in your life. I plead with you, just don't give up on what I have spoken for your life, keep believing until it happens. I have a burning desire to perform My word in your life; but in My timing My word shall fully come to pass. Don't allow your flesh or the Devil to cause you to speak evil of me, wait with Godly integrity. My word precedes Me; whatever I say, I will do. Just know you are not alone right now. The lover of your soul is with you, go ahead fall into your lover's arms (Jesus) and cry, cry until you have no more tears and no sound is coming out of your mouth, I understand. I see your future trading your present tear and frustration for laughter and joy. My love, you know I can't lie, please let those words comfort you as I whisper them so softly in your ear. Stay with me, don't run into another's arms, let Me hold you close and give you My strength. I promise you My word will come true. When I speak, I am never guessing and hoping it will happen. I do not meet with a board to get a vote to see if they agree, no! When I say it, it's done. I'm getting to make you smile.

I Love You

Melonda A. Pace

Dear isolated one,

*S*atan has declared war on the oneness in the church, as well as in our homes. It would be an unnecessary hardship if there wasn't oneness in anything. Paul said, *"I beseech you, brethren, by the name of our Lord Jesus Christ, that ye all speak the same thing and that there be no divisions among you; but that ye be perfectly joined together in the same mind and in the same judgment"*. (I Corinthians 1:10).

Strive patently with all that's within Me to live in harmony with one another. Notice I said that's within Me, Jesus, because I already know My creation (not trying to trick you). I just want you to know how important it is to have oneness, and it can only be done through Me, allow Me to live it through you.

A people can obtain anything when they are one, because communication is flowing sweetly. Communication is understanding, and when you understand, you can act properly, and proper action brings progress.

These things and more are the demolition process that will quickly destroy oneness: pride, a lying tongue, a heart that devises wicked imaginations, feet that are swift in running to mischief, and one that sows discord among the brethren.

Perhaps you can do your job sufficiently by yourself; but if you ask another's help, you will have shown unity, love, and taught someone else what you know, all in oneness. It works; My Father, the Holy Spirit, and I, Jesus Christ, have proven it. (1Peter3:8)

God of Oneness

Dear searching for love,

Real love is waiting for you; no, not a love with dissimulations, rather my heart is open for you to see the real affections I have for you. The nature of My love is so powerful that you will barely be able to stand it in your mortal body. My motives are all pure, I want to take you beyond where you are right now. My love is ready to take you where airplanes can't fly, sorrow can't abide and death is obsolete. My love will be a permanent smile on your face because you will always forever be at your peak. My love died for you before you even heard of Me. Perhaps right now you don't even believe I'm real like so many others; but, My love still wants you. What you're searching for is in Me, Jesus Christ! My love is stellar. I'm not sure if you know that there's another man trying so desperately to keep you from Me; but, make no mistake, his love is dissimulated, he has many disguises, his words are sweet with a bitter end, the wealth he can give you, your life is the price for eternal damnation. His name is Satan, he's smooth, but he's not silk, he's a prince, but he's not supreme. I am the Prince of Peace. Dear Searching, search no longer, I am He you've been so desperately looking for.

True Love
Jesus your Everything.

Ladies!

I'm not going to sugar-coat this at all, we have had enough of that! I bring the naked truth, and for those that can't handle it, turn to another page. Ladies, it's so natural to desire the touch of a natural man's hand. No matter how full your spiritual side may be, it doesn't take away how I created you. Everybody wants to be loved, a real women wants the love of a real man, and vice versa!!!!! You can't pray it away, you can't shower it away, you can't preach it away, you can't fast it away; it's not going anywhere until you die.

Don't be ashamed, it's a wonderful thing. To my ladies who have experienced God's best of men, and no longer have him for what ever reason, God is here for you; He will carry you through the rigorous moments, but first you must give it to Him. God is not going to erase your memory, (laugh out loud). For the ladies that are yet waiting, be encouraged, God has not forgotten you. He's too "God" for that. In the meantime, treasure yourself as God brings forth the rare jewel (man) he has for your treasure box.

All of you have distinguished characteristics you must have in a man. Perhaps it's how he truly listens to you, the thoughtfulness of bringing you flowers "just because", opening your door, or the way he looks at you every time you get up and walk, things that make you want to love him more.

Never forget that Jesus "the man" is here for you, and there is nothing too private for him to handle. He is the God of all flesh, He is able to keep all that you commit unto Him (2 Timothy 1: 12). God will be faithful in everything.

The God of all Flesh

Believing Hard!

Dear servant,

I know you believe everything you've read and heard preached about Me. I know because I see your heart. I know it looks like what I've done for others will not happen for you. The simple necessities in life seem hard for you to obtain in your believing life.

I've heard your earnest prayers, I see that you are faint, but I can see you still believe as you fall to your knees in tears. Yes, you're are experiencing 2 Corinthians 4:8, 9. You are troubled on every side, yet not distressed; you are perplexed, but not in despair; persecuted, but not forsaken; cast down, but not destroyed.

No, you are not losing your mind, you are not doing anything wrong, neither have you missed Me. You are living the above scripture. Your human frame can't bare it, your human mind can't understand why you've done all you know to do, yet things are not changing. Oh, but it is dear one, it's the testing of your faith in Me, so, fall out if you must, but fall in the arms of a rewarding God (Me) the Creator of everything. I send my Son to you today with good news; which is, your life is about to change for the better. Every prophecy is about to come to pass, money is about to over-flow, it's about to be pressed down, shaken together, and it will still be running over any second now per order of our Father in heaven! This is what believing hard perpetually brings forth. Now go encourage someone else. For you overcome by word of testimony.

God

The Race

Dear runner,

Let's compare a natural race, every person has their lane, they are all running toward the finish line. There are some that run a 100 yard dash, 200 yard dash, others run less, there are some who run and jump over hurdles at the same time; yet, they are all running towards the finish line.

Sometimes in training for the race, an athlete may become injured; yet, they still get up the day of the race and prepare to run because they want to cross the finish line.

I've seen some get a cramp while running; but their mind is set on finishing, so they keep running; I'm shouting from the stadium bleachers in heaven, telling you to keep moving. If you can't run any longer, walk. If you can't walk then crawl. If you can't crawl any longer, don't panic, My son Jesus has been running your race with you all the time, and He's ready to carry you across the finish line because you endured until the end.

No, you weren't the fastest runner, not even third to cross the finish line; but you crossed it with My glory upon you. Well done my good and faithful servant!

*From
Your Life Coach
God*

Dear servant,

1 Corinthians 1:27 states, *"But I (God) have chosen the foolish things of the world to confound the wise".* I believe men would understand this better than women. This is a true story. A distinguished gentleman was not shy of having any woman he wanted. If he pursued her, he won her affection. He truly enjoyed the pleasures of women of all fashions.

This distinguished gentleman loves coffee; he has enjoyed a cup of coffee when dining with each beautiful woman. But, there was one women he dated regularly, and she noticed how many packets of sugar he used in his coffee. One day he ordered his cup of coffee and she picked up the packets of sugar, poured it in his coffee and stirred it for him. He was confounded by her simple action ever since that day.

Let's say women are ice cream to keep it simple. There are many flavors, and you can add whatever sweet treats you want to your ice cream to make it taste even better!

On that day she rose above any woman he had met or would ever meet. There are many gods in this fallen world. They can bring many different flavors to try and make your life better; but I, God, am the sugar and the real sweetener in your life. Oh taste and see how good I am. *"How sweet are thy words unto my taste, sweeter than honey to my mouth!"* (Psalm 119:103)

How sweet it is to be Loved by Me

Jesus Christ

Melonda A. Pace

Oh how I love you sweetheart, let Me count the ways:

1. I left My royal place in heaven
2. I became mere flesh
3. I suffered gruesomely for you
4. I allowed bad men to kill Me
5. I overcame death because I love you
6. I give you new mercies daily
7. There are so many more ways in My Word

Don't ever say again that no one loves you. For the Greatest One loves you; now get up and love yourself. Return My love by giving Me your life. **John 3:16** and **Romans 10:9** will lead you in the right direction. If you have already given Me your life, stop questioning and live!

I Love you
God

Dear pastors,

$\mathcal{P}$astors, don't lose your enthusiasm. You may have been doing your job for forty years, and over half of your congregation may be 3 to 5 years in their walk with God. Teach with great compassion, preach with a conviction, love with pure hearts and never cease to ask Me for a refreshing word,

You don't have to feed My people yesterday's bread. Many of you are so lost in being the pastor of a mega-ministry, as well as pastoring in multi locations that you have forgotten you are My servant. Get your focus back, God is depending on you to edify the Christian world. Motivate them to hold on and witness to others until I come, **which will be very soon**. I need to be the center of attraction again.

Many of you haven't realized that I have left your sanctuary a long time ago. I'm in the parking lot, waiting to be invited back. Come to Me that I may fill you with new wine for the new movement of our Father, just before he sends Me to rapture His saints.

I love you all, and I salute you for your "yes" to Me. Many didn't answer the call. Great is your reward for your "yes". I'm just asking the pastors whom I've called to take time and check their voice mail. I've been calling but had to leave messages.

The Son of God
Jesus Christ

Dear ready to die,

hy do you think death is best for you? Why are you trying so hard to die? You don't yet know the complete thoughts I have for you. If you die now, I won't be able to say "well done".

You can't die in your process. I am here to be incredibly strong for you. For some reason, you think you are alone in your trials; but you are not, you are not the first one to be divorced, hated, falsely accused, or have a love one die.

Whatever your situation may be, I want you to know that you still have a reason to live. Don't attempt suicide. God has a great plan for your life.

Yes, you may be in the pit right now; but you are only a few steps from the palace. You've come too far, you've prayed so long, you've paid too great a price to give up now. My sister and my brother, you still have something to live for.

Maybe it's been a cloudy time for you; but there is a silver lining. There are sunny years to come. If it means anything to you, Jesus is on your side; and He's fighting for you. Just don't die now; because there is so much good ahead.

Be encouraged
J. C.

BE YOU!

To My one-of-a-kind,

*D*on't change because I love you the way you are. I made you just the way I wanted you to be. Whatever your nationality, that is exactly designed you.

It doesn't matter if you're tall, short, red hair, blond hair, wide nose, pointed nose, slanted eyes, big eyes, etc. That's what I wanted you to be. Don't envy anyone else because you really admire their appearance. Don't try to get as many degrees as the next person. Be educated, but don't provoke unhealthy competition between yourself and others.

Maybe you can't do math in your head, maybe you need paper and pencil, and 30 minutes, and still come up with the wrong answer. Celebrate the mathematically inclined, you are no less of a person. I made, and gave you precisely what I intended you to be.

The number 8 can never be 100; but, if you add 10, 30, 50, and 2 with 8, together they make 100. Even though they are shaped differently, their value is equal in the end. You are valuable to Me in this world, I need you to help Me make up the difference.

Be confident in what I have given you

God

The flesh,

My Love, come let us reason together. Don't be dismayed about your flesh. It is always going to be true to itself, "*in the flesh dwelleth no good thing*" (Romans 7:18-22). So stop being shocked when bad thoughts come to your mind. It may be for good reasons to the flesh that you slap someone; but, you Can't yield to your flesh all the time. Yes, I said "all the time", for there are sweet and beautiful things that are profitable to our flesh. "*For this cause shall a man leave his father and mother, and shall be joined together unto his wife, and they shall be one flesh*" (Ephesians 5:31). A married man and woman giving fleshly pleasure to one another, oh how sweet it is. For this is the time to please the flesh.

Behold, I am the Lord, the God of all flesh. There is nothing too hard for Me, I am able to keep your flesh from doing thoughtless things, I'm able to pour out My spirit upon all flesh. Give your flesh to Me, let Me show you how amazing I can be in your flesh. My Love, do you really understand that you struggle not against flesh and blood; but against evil spirits you can't see, against powers, and the rulers of darkness in this world. There is so much wickedness in the earth, and I want so badly to protect you because I love you so much.

Your flesh and heart can fail you at any given moment fighting alone; but I want to be your portion of strength. I want to be your heartbeat forever. I need to be pleased by you, but you can't do it in your flesh. I want to be fulfilled inside of you.

Come naked before Me, My love, that I may clothe you with My whole armor that you may be able to stand in these evil days. I want to protect you against the evil one that's trying to desperately still, kill, and destroy your life every second he gets. Please give Me your flesh. I know you desire to do good, but evil is always present. (Galatians 5:17-26)

Melonda A. Pace

Dear servant,

Many of us use excuses to justify our failings. Do you know that you have an obligation to walk down the path I, God, has prepared for you? This is why you're are here on earth, for I have a purpose for the life I gave you.

It may be a fact that you're not the best singer, dancer, rapper, news anchor, lawyer or doctor. But I need you to be, no, not be the best, but be (meaning to exist), to take your place in this world, live your life according to My will. Excuses are always available, but you can find courage in Me to say "no more excuses". God has given Me reasons to put away My excuses.

I hear you say "well you know I didn't finish school, I'm not as smart as they are". I'm not asking you to be as smart as they are, I want you to be as smart as I am, God! Therefore, I place before you an option: are you going to keep your mountain of excuses or will you allow Me to show you how clever I can be in your life? After all, my history is astounding! I made water flow from a rock, I made a shepherd boy a mighty king and I created the world in 6 days. It's so easy to make excuses; but it's very unselfish to say "no more excuses", I'm going to be a beacon of light for someone else. Because believe it or not, someone is watching you, you are a role model to someone else's eyes. It could be that child in your neighborhood or someone that attends your church. It could be someone you speak to casually every day. If I can get each person to realize that their life is not their own, maybe people will stop making excuses.

God

Melonda A. Pace

Suicide

My child,

*D*on't commit suicide on the road to your destiny; more than anything, I want you to make it. I want to see the satisfaction on your face when you make it to your destiny. Sometimes one gets so excited about what God has revealed to them, they make a common mistake that can be deadly.

In the 13th chapter of 1 Kings a servant of mine made four mistakes and lost his life. It's so heart-breaking, but it didn't have to happen. First, he talked too much; second, he was found in the wrong place; third, he became vulnerable and fourth, he was disobedient, after obeying God.

Everyone who jumps and smiles with you, are not always on your side. If you ask Me for the spirit of discernment, I would gladly reveal these things to you. I don't want to make you sad, but I just want to encourage you to be wise, happy, and vigilant.

There are spies in your life; there are things you may be tied to that are draining the life out of your destiny. My servant, in this story, listened to cunning words of deception with his ears, and not with his heart (spirit). Don't allow people to make you feel bad about what God is doing for you. People will get close just to discover My great plans for you, just to stop you by any means necessary.

God

To Whom it concerns,

(The writer of this book is speaking)

*D*on't give up! That's my prayer for you. I notice you're living in an Extended Stay Hotel, making less than $300 a week, with a child to raise. Your rent is $286, a week, I know that strenuous. There is another, living in their car with 3 children, literally, waking up and going to school and work from their car! There are many that share the same story, as well as others that are beneath, and it appears life is not going to get any better.

Well, I declare to you this day that your life is about to be so much better. Keep on looking up, heaven is working on your behalf. I don't know the reasons that brought you here, but I do know a God that is able to bring you out. I may not know you personally, but it doesn't stop me from believing and hoping for you, that's what the love of God does inside imperfect man.

(From another human being who's been there; and knows God will deliver you.)

Be so Encouraged

Dear Lord,

(A child's question): I do not like my life right now. Why did my mother kill herself? I didn't ask to come here, but here I am, now without a mother, also without a father. He's not dead, he just doesn't want to have anything to do with me, this makes my little heart so sad. This place I'm in is a terrible place. I feel so alone, even around other family members who love me. It looks like there is no God anywhere, and there is no one to whom I can express just how I feel. Why is this happening? You see Lord, I'm in this world but, where is my hope? Not for tomorrow, but the next hour. I'm in this world, but where is my peace of mind? I'm in this world, but where is the love that conquers all? I'm in this world, but where is the joy unspeakable?

(God's response): Oh suffering one from life's mishaps, I hear your question, and I feel your pain, believe me I do. I ask you to gently trust Me in this place. Yes, you're in this world; and I am the answer to every one of your questions, just trust Me in this place. I, God, promise you if you trust Me I will give you wings to fly like an eagle. You will witness joy unspeakable, hope that fulfills, and I will cover you with My blanket of peace. I'm so sorry you had to go through all of these things, but through the years you will find that all this was working for your good. Last but not least, I want you to know I wrote these scriptures for wonderful people like you in mind. Psalm 27:10, Proverbs 3:5,6

God

Dear servant,

*S*weet, wonderful, willing worker, you are so faithful to your church, you are committed to your job, you are the best usher, nurse, choir member, pastor, youth director, deacon, member. You are wonderful in all of these things. Don't stop being a willing worker, for every church needs people like you; but, you are yet to have a relationship with Me, God. I just want to entice you to begin a relationship with Me, God.

Love You Dearly

To My high achievers,

I applaud you who have achieved in this earthly world. You possess many things, houses in different countries, personal jets, and several degrees. Oh how you have fulfilled every one of your plans, congratulations! I can relate, for I am also a high achiever.

I humbly want you to know, everything you've used, I've given to you. The constituent power of your brain; the atoms and protons in each nucleus, all those phenomenal possessions, I, God created them.

There's a King in the Bible by the name of King Nebuchadnezzar, he became a little confused with his achievements; but, he came to himself and acknowledged Me.

The greatest thing you can ever achieve isn't hard at all and doesn't require entering another college for another four years. It's as simple as asking Me to come into your heart. One lives on earth only so many years with their wealth and accomplishments, then they all perish.

But, with Me, after this life on earth, you can live forever and be richer far beyond what you've experienced here. Lawyers, you can't articulate or negotiate well enough; doctors, you can't prescribe a medication; philosophers, your logic and reason can't satisfy; scientist, you can't put Me in a test tube to extract knowledge. It's as simple as asking Me to come into your life. I will make you so better, you can't even begin to imagine.

The Master of Everything
Jehovah

Dear cherished one,

*D*on't let the inner you become the enemy; don't let being afraid stop you from living your dream. The Lord is your light, to brighten your path, and your salvation. Whom shall you fear? The Lord is the strength of your life so don't be afraid.

When Jesus came to earth, He didn't come thinking maybe He could do everything the Father had given Him. His mind was already set; I must do the will of Him that sent me. I just want to encourage you to let Jesus' mind be in you (Philippians 2:5).

Can you do it? Yes you can! Don't stop if it doesn't work as well as you thought the first time. Take a moment to pray and ask God to reveal the problem, and how he can make it better. If you give up now, later will be more of the same. Why? Because you gave into fear, and stopped trying. So keep pushing toward your goals in this life and the life to come.

Listen, in working out your goals you may get butterflies in your stomach, but make them fly like an eagle above the storm! Your knees may begin to wobble, but don't fall down.

Yes you can!
God

A Living Praise

Dear servant,

Even though you have seen too much to doubt God, there are times when your heart is overwhelmed, because the facts of life are combating your faith to live, which raises ordinary questions in your mind; such as:

How do I wait like Job in this life?

How do I kill my giants like David?

How do I obey God like Noah, in this life, when I haven't had a sign in years that it's going to rain?

How do I pack my things and go like Abraham, not knowing where I'm going?

You must learn to live in the power of praise. There is wisdom and dialogue in praise, the wisdom is knowing when you praise, I will come. Therefore you have brought God on the scene; now there is opportunity for dialogue between you and God.

Your praise says to Me, "I trust you with my life, even if I don't quite understand what's going on this very minute. I know you hold me in Your care, and You're not going to let anything happen to me that isn't necessary for my good".

When you sincerely praise; God speedily appears and begins possessing your situation because God's power is forever living. It's still in existence; it's not destroyed, lost or extinct, but it's brings forth glorification in life.

If you praise Me, I will come

God!

Dear servant,

" *For* unto us was the gospel preached, as well as unto them: but the word preached did not profit them, not being mixed with faith in them that heard it." (Hebrews 4:2)

The table is set. The linen table cloth and crisp linen napkins are laid over a beautiful cherry oak table with the finest china, solid gold utensils and Australian crystal goblets which line the table. This well-dressed table is fit for a king and queen. It is symbolic to the Word of God the Bible.

The table is set; but there is no food. The bread of life is not being fused with faith. *"And all things, whatsoever ye shall ask in prayer, believing, ye shall receive."* (Matthew 21:22)

So many of you are only sitting at the table adoring its beauty; yet you are dying from malnutrition. There isn't a famine in the land; but, intermittent faith. Intermittent faith is when you believe that God forgave your sins, and He's coming back one day — and that's the limit of your faith.

You must extend your faith to Gods ability; and there is never, anything too hard for God, (Luke 1:37). I challenge you today, to grasp your faith (whether it's preposterous, contrary to nature, reason, or common sense). As you fuse your faith with God's word, the table will be filled. Faith is a fundamental element

Melonda A. Pace

that's essential for the fusion of the Word of God to become a reality in this life.

Let's Feast on You Faith
God

Dear reader

(The writer of this book is speaking),

*A*nother morning I wake up to not enough, I don't have enough money to take care of the small necessities of life; oh how this makes my heart ache so, until it hurts for me to breath.

Another morning I must face my child as if we have not a problem in the world. I'll be making breakfast for the rest of the day; because all I have are eggs, bread, and juice.

I boiled the eggs this morning. For lunch, I'll scramble them. At dinner, I will make them sunny-side up. Honestly, every month when it's time for my rent to be paid, it's as if God performs the miracle at the Red Sea once again. Can any body feel what I'm saying?

Yesterday was Sunday. I praised God for abundance in my life. The pastor's message was — believe! Listen people, for many years I have awoken to not enough; but, every evening I have laid down and I still believe! Keep believing my friend, as I believe with you

(He promised us a morning's of joy, Psalm 30:5 J)

Melonda A. Pace

The Test

Dearest one,

I'm curious about some things. Are you able to trust Me? If I blindfold your eyes, will you still walk the path? When My footprints have been removed, tell me, will you still believe My dear? I, God, said when you exit the church doors, will you enter faith doors. The Word you heard must be activated in the world.

Can you past the test? Will you give Me your best? Are you willing to travail until my Word is fulfilled? Are you willing to wait on Me until I'm ready to perform My word in your life? Will you still minister to others when trouble is present in your life?

When it looks like I'm a liar in doubters eyes, will you stand assured knowing it's impossible for your God to lie? I am counting on you, dearest one, to make Me look good. You might be thinking, you don't have what it takes; but I want you to know you have it. I put in you, I'm just waiting on you to discover the greatness inside of you to ace the test.

Never Forget I Love You
God

Dear servant,

nce you've experienced real love, a counterfeit love will never please you. After you've had a taste of real love, a watered down love will never satisfy. God in heaven is the creator of real love, and I want you to have it in your life.

Real love never stops giving, it only gets better at doing it over and over again; even if it goes six feet under, it never dies, it searches for another heart in which to live.

Sweetness, real love is so powerful; it will bring light to the darkest place in your life. Real love is so intense. Love races to your deepest hurt, real love covers your imperfections until you get yourself together. Just open your heart to God and let Me show you real love, and how to share it with someone else.

When mankind experiences the real love of God, and truly understands it, they will never settle for a man or women that doesn't have the attributes of My real love. I see you troubled in your mind, crazy love has got you so blind. The one you're loving has told you that you're not worth a dime; but for some reason, you're thinking one day he/she will change their mind.

It's the real love that I have for you. Real love is going to change that dime they said you're worth into a gold mine. My love is ready to take you to heights unknown

Bad experiences have made you cautious of the most beautiful thing in the world—which is love. The feeling of being in love is magnificent, it's a great tragedy not to have it in your life. Love is the most wonderful thing to experience, beside salvation and Christ.

He Kept You Alive (a poem from the author)

Dear friend,

We never know what's going to happen
The very next second in our lives
Yet we plan, hope, and expect it to work in our favor
Truly we never know

We never know when it will be our very last time
To say the words I love you
Be encouraged my sister and my brother
Truly we never know

We never know when we will experience another
September 11
Many lost their lives, others was beneath the world
Trade Center
Where God miraculously fought death for their life
And He kept them alive!

Many things have happened in and around your life
You know it was over for you, and you're wondering today
How did it turn out the way it did, you know you should
be dead, but

He kept you alive for a purpose
He kept you alive to give him glory
He kept you alive so you can smile again
He kept you alive to be a living testimony

Go tell someone else what God has done for you

An Exhausted Yes

Dear friend

(from the author),

*R*ealizing I've been stuck on stupid a long time, truly in reality I was boxing God. I knew my arms were too short to get a punch in, my mind wasn't smart enough to out think Him. I couldn't find a lawyer to negotiate the right words, because all God wanted to hear was my yes. One day, I understood that the many things I've been waiting for God to fulfill, the struggles that I no longer want to have, all depend on me saying "yes" to the Lord.

I've been waiting for many prophesies to be fulfilled. I get fiery angry with God because they haven't happened yet and I'm old (lol), well, I must confess I have spent most of my time in the ring boxing God!

This letter is my neon red flag in the middle of the road waving to the reader, STOP! I scream with love, it's only a waste of precious time.

Now I realize saying "yes" to God has changed my condition for the better. For you it may be a church He told you to join. However, you don't want to go because your family has been in your current church for 50 years. Whatever your circumstance, you know what God wants you to say "yes" to. I desperately beg you to say "yes" to the Lord. Your "yes" tells the Lord "I agree with you concerning the will You have for my life, and I truly repent to You, God. I realize that if

You have prepared it for me, You have <u>designed </u>the strength, peace, wisdom, tolerance, joy, love…everything that I will need."

Ready to Work with God
Melonda

Dear friend

(a letter from the author),

I am guilty of falling out with God, protesting by staying home from church, resigning from my position, because I had a major attitude with God. I began to think for a brief moment that He was playing games with me.

He was toying with me, He was taking advantage of my feelings, and He was minimizing the importance of my needs. My thinking was so wrong! Yet, His mercy was new for me every morning, with Him knowing I was going to get up and continue to act a like a fool.

I was so done with God , thinking I could escape Him if I didn't go to church; I could think negative about Him in my mind and He not know, and thinking I can make it on my own strength.

People, God is inescapable; He is omnipresent, He is everywhere with His whole being at the same time; He is omnipotent, all powerful, there is no strength greater than His. God is omniscient, all knowing, He knows what we are going to think before we think it.

We can't afford to think of God as being frivolous and feeble-minded, it is a waste of time; I know I'm not the first to think this way and won't be the last.

Satan came to convince us the way he did and one-third of the angels in heaven fell. Satan is a master deceiver; don't ever think you can stand against him and his demons on your own, they will beat you to a pulp in 10 seconds. We must negate this poisonous thinking quickly, and ask God to forgive us immediately. And remember, you can never lose God because He is inescapable.

Dear Sheep,

*S*t. John 10:4,5 says "...and the sheep follow him: for they know his voice. And a stranger will they not follow, but will flee from him: for they know not the voice of strangers. I am the good shepherd: the good shepherd giveth his life for the sheep." This letter is not about all people being your enemy, but it's telling you to be cautious of the those you love dearly and look up to, and vise -versa.

They could so easily give you advice to do the opposite of what God has told you do, simply because they don't think God meant for you to do a certain thing. If you heed to them instead of God, it will be harmful to you. We must learn to take God at His word.

Learn to detect the voice of the enemy. It may come from a loving parent, a sister or brother, or your best friend. I'm not asking you to excommunicate them; but learn My voice versus the enemy's voice. Because the enemy will use whomever to side-track you, and the person is not aware of it most of the time.

Our enemies don't play fair at all, he truly comes to still kill and destroy all of the things that I (God) have for you. It is a must that you get to know me my precious one.

God has infinite ways to bless you, but you're stuck on one way.

Dear Love Ones,

Death is the most problematical thing you have to come across in this life. For whatever the cause may be, old age, accident, suicide, no matter how it occurs, they all share the same reality that a loved one is no longer present on this earth.

You can't call them and say "I'm going to the mall, would you like to ride with me?" You can't hear your mom or dad's voice again to soothe your heart. After they've been gone for years, instinct and unfathomable love will cause the impulse to pick up the phone and call someone that no longer resides in this wretched world, but now lives in a perfect place.

One would say don't cry, I say why not cry, for it's My expression of love. Some would say you don't need to be alone, but I say why not, because some of us have friends like Job, clueless of what to say. Therefore, let Me comfort you with these words. The hurt in your heart will become lighter as moments pass; but the fact that your loved ones are gone will always be a reality.

Remember <u>as I go with you through this process</u>, don't shut Me out, don't become bitter with Me, because I took back what belonged to Me from the beginning. I only shared them with you for a little while. I am here to carry you through this most difficult time in your life.

God Who Cares

Melonda A. Pace

Dear failure,

Failure in life causes you to become a spectacle, but with God it brings you to the front of the line, that's when God knows you need him the most.

"*How think ye? If a man have a hundred sheep, and one of them be gone astray, doth he not leave the ninety and nine, and goeth into the mountains, and seeketh that which is gone astray? And if so be that he find it, verily I say unto you, he rejoiceth more of that sheep, than of the ninety and nine which went not astray. If a man will do this for his sheep, you best believe I will do the same for you, my sheep, for I am the Good Shepherd.*" (Matthew 18:12, 13)

Take My hand and arise from the failure, trust in Me, don't be discouraged, I have the power to heal and rebuild because in Me there is no failure. People will continue to talk, but listen to Me; people will push you away, but press into Me; for I am more than the entire universe against you!

Even if you brought this failure upon yourself; I will yet restore you and bring you to the place I desire you to be, <u>because I refuse to take My hands off of you.</u>

I am Failure Coverage
God

Dear servant,

What if the life you have lived up to this point is as good as it gets? Single people, you may never get married; or the multi- millionaire may never bless you like God told him to and you are hoping for it so strongly.

I don't force My will on anyone; you must freely obey and follow Me. Honestly, what if I spoke to you right now and said this is as good as it's going to get. You will always have just enough finances to get by, you can't rob Peter to pay Paul because they are both broke!

What if the change you're expecting will never come, war will be always, no peace, that's a devastating thought; but this is true for those that don't believe in Me, or a heaven or hell. For those people, this is as good as it gets. This is the only heaven they will experience; but, for those who have accepted Jesus Christ in their hearts; heaven awaits, much more beautiful and peaceful beyond this world. Stay with God no matter what.

Heaven Belongs to You
Jesus Christ

Dear servant,

Many of us miss the most wonderful moments in life. Like watching a bride walk down the isle to her man who is looking at her as if life can't get any sweeter.

It catches you off guard, like sitting in your bay window seat after the rain, when suddenly the clouds move away from the sun which shines warmly on your face. That is God's spot light on you, as if there is no one else in the world.

The rain drops on the window pane and the splendor of grass glistens as the warm sun rays shine on them as if God rained down rubies, emeralds, and diamonds at your feet. Then in the sky, enhancing the sun is God's covenant, the rich colors of a rainbow accenting the rain drops of jewels.

It's Divine moments in time that relax your racing mind, in these moments you shouldn't speak a word, just sit there and let the wonderfulness of this divine moment speak to you.

Take Time Enjoy The Masterpieces I Draw With My Finger Of Love For You

God

Obesity

Dear cherished one,

I love you do much, and I care about every part of you, perhaps the vicissitude of life brought you to this point, whatever avenue brought you to this point, don't panic, we can make it better together.

Allow me to put my super to your natural, and we can make things better for you. I don't want your health to be poor, because I have so much ministry for you to do. Will you trust me to make it better, allow me to change your habits and diet, don't say you can't do it, my word is true, and there is nothing to hard for me.

My super natural power can work wonders in your body quickly, things that take years to do I can go against all the rules. Take time to talk to me, I have the power to take the very things you crave that isn't good for you, come, lets walk and talk together, ride a bike with me on a country road lined with beautiful oak trees, lets work this out together.

Dear fiend

(a letter from the author),

One summer morning I was lying in bed with the fresh morning air blowing through my slightly open window, temperature just right from a nights rain. With my arms wrapped around my soft pillow holding it tightly, I asked God, "What's so good about waiting" it is not the first thing on anyone's list to do, yet You made it inevitable. He spoke to me so calmly, and begin to say, "It's not a punishment, it is preparatory and wisdom; waiting is preparation to handle what's coming, and wisdom teaches you how to keep it forever. Then He said to me, it makes you transparent. Look that word up He said to me, moving from my comfortable position I reached for the dictionary, I read that "transparent" means transmitting light so that objects on the other side can be seen clearly. He expressed, I shine My light from My side through your souls, the inner you, and if you could stop complaining, you can see clearly you're not ready for marriage, pastorship, to start your business just yet, so, when you really look at it you're making Me wait too. I am waiting on you to comply to My will, then He told me to look up waiting, which means to be prepared or ready; so if I have you waiting you are not ready. The best way to deal with waiting is to be a gentleman and a lady and yield gracefully to it as in

saying thank you for holding me back from making
my life a disaster. Consider waiting your best friend.

Jesus Christ

Melonda A. Pace

Dear Humankind

(from the author),

We are imitations, whatever greatness comes from us; it's all God, whether you believe or not, it doesn't change its truth!

Melonda Pace

Brought Out!

Dear servant,

My child, I am proving you, I am trying you by fire, for I have ordained this season of famine in your life. At one point you were almost consumed by the fire, but I... many days you almost drown in the water, but I ... you said to yourself out of weariness, I'm going to give up because I can't take it any longer, but I... You were looking at others around you, that refused to take me as their Lord and Savior, living better than you, riding in the best cars, living in the biggest houses, wearing the latest fashion, and the lack of money seems to never be a problem in their life, but I...brought you out into a wealthy place.

Now I speak to you who are going through your proving time, think it not strange. For this is God's way of testing our faith and the love we say we have for Him. Don't give up before your appointed time to be brought out; be strong my sister, oh, hold on my brother, for God has not forgotten any of us. He knows your house address, where you shop, work, where you get your pedicure woman, where you get your hair cut man! I am telling you, no matter where you are in this world, when it's time for you to be brought out into your wealthy place; he knows where to find you. (Selah) Psalm 66

Melonda A. Pace

IT'S HARD

Dear servant,

It's hard, you say but I want you to know it's not excusable. Did I, Jesus Christ, tell you that it would be so easy for you? Better yet, do you think it was easy for me, Jesus Christ? I hear that millions of times an hour and I deem it true, but it does not give you the entitlement to give in to indiscretions! The woman says her weakness is men, the man say his weakness is women, the drug addict says his weakness is drugs, the drug dealer says his weakness is the ravenous addict, it's a cycle of exploit.

I have prearranged strength for you to press toward the mark of higher living and thinking. Sometimes it's hard because you're making it harder than it has to be; (example) when you can't answer your phone and talk freely because you don't know which man or woman you're talking to, so you have to be careful not to say the wrong thing or call the wrong name.

Looking over your shoulder so many times, the person that's with you at the moment thinks you have a nerve problem. That's not living, that's constantly running scared, and that's hard. If you are always running you don't have time to walk and smell the roses. You are living in a fallen world, granted. There are so many bad choices to make; but, there are good choices as well. Don't bow down to hardship, because it's use to winning the battle. I encourage you to turn your back on it and stand face-to-face to someone that's conquered this hardship.

Jesus Christ,

P.S, (I'm not say, that doing good will keep hard intervals away, they come to make you strong, don't add to the hardship by doing brainless things.)

Dear Zombies

(a letter from the author)

*M*ake Up! You are born into this damned world with and enemy, even though when you were born, you didn't know anyone; but, somebody knew you. He is so evil that he is trying to kill you, and you haven't done any thing to merit this attack.

Please understand, this is not going to change. Every birthday, he's going to be there, bringing venomous gifts. Every success you have, he will be there to try to tear it down. Perhaps you are beginning to understand the word <u>assigned,</u> this enemy is not going anywhere. Don't panic, God sent a super-hero into the world just for your assigned enemy; his name is Jesus Christ

Dear bitter,

I understand you were exceedingly disappointed by someone or something in time; but one must never, ever allow the door of bitterness to open in their heart. Bitterness is a strong drink that will have you spending your life stone drunk.

It will cause you to be resentful to God, man, family, friends, the cat, dog, and even people you don't know. Bitterness is self destruction, it smothers love and gives life to hate.

Hate contaminates your thinking, it's so powerful you'll begin to think you are the only one in the world that's right. You will think you know better than God. You will think everyone is out to get you. Well dear, stop, sit down and think, have you ever disappointed someone before? Did you want forgiveness?

Let Me love you out of this toxic state. Set your affection on things above, not things on the earth. Let Me show you how to handle bitter disappointment with My sweet love. *"…we are more than conquerors through him that loved us."* (Romans 8:37)

The Lover of Your Soul
Jesus Christ

Melonda A. Pace

Dear Students of Life

Proverbs 22:6 says "*Train up a child in the way he should go: and when he is older, he will not depart from it.*" To my students, who are called from this point on as, parents and children; if you follow my instructions you will not fail this class.

Journey means to travel from one place to another. Parents, after your child is born, you expect progression in your child. If you fail to see this, your first thought is something is wrong, and you take them to the doctor to seek the problem.

Children, you are not born adults, you must become one. You can have all the material to build a house; but if you know not how to build it correctly, it will be a disaster. The solid foundation for your house is parental teaching. You must go through the process, and you will not be skipped to another grade.

Parents, teach your children well as I teach you. Children, learn the lessons well, and when it's time for you to take your journey, remember what your parents taught you.. You all have built a solid and beautiful house together; now live in it with Me. I will not depart from you.

Remember, someone allowed you to take your journey.

In My Love
God

CONSTITUENTS OF THE WORLD:

Dear friend

(a letter from the author),

 he way to greatness is humbleness; "*Let this mind be in you, which was also in Christ Jesus; who, being in the form of God thought it not robbery to be equal with God: But made himself of no reputation, and took upon him the form of a servant, and was made in the likeness of man: and being found in fashion as a man, he humbled himself, and became obedient unto death, even the death of the cross. Wherefore God also hath highly exalted him, and given him a name which is above every name.*" (Philippians 2:5-11)

I consider myself to be better than no one and the least of everyone. There isn't anything wrong with desiring and reaching for greatness; but we must keep it in perspective. There is no need to trample over anyone or annihilate their name to achieve greatness. If it's to be, the Lord will graciously escort you to that platform. Jesus made his entrance on a donkey into Jerusalem, which is considered the lowest of its kind. I was told to be careful of how you treat people going up, because you may meet and need them on the way down.

But we all can start practicing greatness right now, by being the greatest bathroom cleaner, empting the trash, vacuuming, dusting, and cutting the grass in our homes and at our church, even at someone else house

Melonda A. Pace

if need be. Loving thy neighbor as thyself, helping others that are in need of food clothes, prayer, and long suffering, rightly divining the word of God, this is the greatness God wants; let us meet the challenge!

In His Love
Melonda

To My dearest child,

I hear the murmuring, and the complaining about your testing. I want to say the testing **I'm taking you through**, but I can't say that because you are so confrontational. You'll ask: Why this? Why me? and How long Lord do I have to deal with this? I can't take you through it until you yield in it.

It hasn't crossed your mind once, that maybe Satan has had a conversation with me about you, like Job. I hear you saying, well, I didn't have all the things that Job had. Lord you see me already living from pillow to post now, what more do you want? Well, I'm glad you asked. I want complete submission.

My dearest child, learn the lesson from Job, as a matter of fact, read the questions I asked him, and I want you to answer them. Have worms made a buffet out of your body, eating at your skin? Do you have painful boils that are running puss from your body? I know you have friends like Job, judgmental, and don't have an inkling of my business because they are to earthly minded, yet they try to speak spiritual.

Take note, Job 23:10 *"But he the knoweth the way that I take: when he has tried me, I shall come forth as gold".* Then read verse 14 *"For he (God) performeth the thing(s) that is appointed for me. My children count it all joy; I know the course I have you on, because I put you there, no, not forever, but until you have become refined gold."*

(Know that everything I take you through will end in <u>pure</u> joy if you stay with Me.)

Your Father in heaven

A Good Report

Dear servant,

Many are the afflictions of the righteous; Steven was stoned, John the Baptist was beheaded, Jesus was crucified, Mary was ridiculed, Paul was shipwrecked, Daniel was thrown in the den of lions, Jonah was in the belly of the whale, David had to run like a fugitive, Silas was locked in jail, Samson's eyes were plucked out, Uriah was murdered, Jeremiah was fearlessly denounced by his family and hometown, and Joseph was put in a pit.

The good report is the sufferings of your present time are not worthy to be compared with the glory which shall be revealed in you. One moment in heaven will pay for all the afflictions you have and will encounter for Christ's sake. We shall live forever, never worrying about afflictions, because there will be none. There will be nothing but joy, peace, and love, and there shall be no more death. We shall live in a perfect world forever!

Jesus Christ

Children of God,

I need you to be so very watchful, of not falling into a coma form. You are so quick to say not me, oh no, I won't do that; but it's possible. I, the Lord, sit high and look below, it can move stealthily upon you before you even realize. You are not wrestling with flesh, but, with a master cunning spirit, it's shrewd.

What's a coma form the Lord? It happens when you become weary in waiting. You are yet working in the vineyard for the Father, preaching, singing, teaching, healing, and praying; but your heart is fainting because you think I have put your personal matters on the back burner; you have slipped into a coma, yet going through the formality of godliness.

I am a God that's concerned about the wholeness of man, every element. You are my people, you chose to serve Me, and that touched My heart, and I love you so much for that. Know that I'm going to take care of every part of you in this life. Don't believe I will do it for someone else and doubt that I will do it for you! I will and I shall! There are pleasures I'm going to give you that are going to blow your mind!

Yours truly,
God of wholeness

THE MATRIX

Dear servant,

The Comforter I left for all that believe in Me is so much more. When you accept Me as your Lord and Savior, I give you supernatural power; meaning the Comforter (The Holy Ghost - The Holy Spirit). He is mystical, ghostly, unusual, and unnatural. And He is all for your utilization. For further information on the Holy Ghost, I have summoned you to meet with Me in the spirit that I may converse with you how vast My spirit is.

God

NOW FAITH

Dear servant,

"Now faith is the substance of things hoped for, the evidence or things not seen." (Hebrews 11:1)

"Take my yoke upon you, and learn of me; for I am meek and lowly in heart; and ye shall find rest unto your souls. For my yoke is easy, and my burden is light." (Matthew 11:29-30)

*D*enotation: Faith in progress is the responsibility of the servants of God. If you're expecting to see immediate and visible proof of faith, you can't, it's not visible. Because you can't see results of faith, you shy away from God; therefore your responsibility to have faith has become a heavy burden.

A yoke is a frame carried between 2 person's shoulders with equal load, when you take part with me, God, I am in the yoke with you. But when you withdraw from Me, your ultimate strength, you make faith in life hard to bare. Job 5:7 has bluntly told you that trouble is already assigned to you.

Dear servant, when you can't see the results of your faith, stay connected to Me (stay in the yoke) because you're connected to the One that's going to bring forth the substance of you faith.

God

From the author

*B*elieving doesn't mean that you will always get what you want. True belief is always counted to you as righteousness in the eyes of God. On earth, we believe God for many things like the healing of love ones from sickness, yet they die. This is not because we didn't truly believe, but because God is sovereign. He can do what he chooses to do, and we don't have the right to be angry with God. You just keep believing, what you believe, that there is nothing God can't do!

There are some things God will not tell you such as the reason He didn't do something. I have come to realize that this is the divine line of God, you can't cross the line. The sooner we come to grips with this the better our minds will be. He never told us that He would give us all the answers, even though He has all the answers. We must learn (as I have today) how to stay in a human's place (as His creation). At no time can we be God and human. We must simply except what God allows and keep believing. We must utilize the heck out of the comforter God left us, let Him comfort you when you don't understand why your million dollar ideas aren't working. Let Him comfort you as to why He allowed a sweet teenager to die at school minutes after her mother dropped her off. I have truly learned to shut my mouth like Job, after all He is God and I am human. I've learned my place, I am the puppet and he is the puppet master.

To My Heart,

I, Jesus Christ, the son of God speak peace to you in you in the fiery furnace, and your lions' den. No, you can't in reality touch or see a real furnace or lion; but metaphorically, you are in highly intense living right now, and to the natural eye it doesn't look favorable to you in the slightest.

I've heard you say, like one of the three Hebrew boys, that I won't deliver you, yet you know that I am able too. How notable this is of you. Allow Me to share a fact with you concerning sowing and reaping. Many things you have sown in this life may not all come to fruition. It's possible that you may not reap all in this life you are in right now, but My word is true, you shall reap.

So don't be discouraged nor confused when children of God have left this life an gone to their heavenly home. You know they suffered greatly for my sake, but didn't receive the magnitude of reaping for their sowing. Take comfort in knowing they shall reap for every pain, and tear.

Now concerning you that remain on earth; suffer for Me well. Therefore, stay confident, for I come quickly; and My reward is with Me, to give every man according as his work. Endure hardness, as a good soldier of Jesus Christ!

Build Your Rewards
Jesus Christ

To Earth's Constituents

(a letter from the author),

I consider myself better than no one, and the least of everyone. As a child I was presented with the true and living God. As an adult I received and believed in this God.

I take no pleasure in unwise debate with whose God is right or wrong; but, I will say, I would love to see the world your gods could create.

In His Love
Melonda Pace

To Whom It May Concern:

Read This Again,

*D*on't cause discomfort in someone else's life, for there is no good you can gain from hurting another. It may seem right at the moment, but in the end there will only be corruption. I see and know all, absolutely nothing gets passed Me. It may seem at the time that many are getting away without any repercussions, but they aren't.

Allow Me to perfect the man in the mirror (You, whom I love dearly), My word (The Bible) teaches mankind not to interfere in other men's matters. Seek to do good to others, even those who mistreat you, let brotherly love continue.

If you must interfere in other people's matters, let it be in secret prayer, praying that I will bless them, even if they have despitefully used you (Matthew 5:44). Dearly beloved, avenge not yourselves; but rather give place unto wrath; for it is written, vengeance is Mine: I will repay, saith the Lord.

Tell the man, woman, boy or girl that's in the mirror to let My (God) reflection show up in them. My spirit can help you discipline yourself <u>in every situation</u>. You must learn to help others, and not try to rule their lives, there is a huge difference.